101 Questions for Humanity

Coffee Table Philosophy

J Edward Neill

Cover Graphic by J Edward Neill

Tessera Guild Publishing

ISBN-13: 978-1508733027
ISBN-10: 1508733023

For armchair philosophers everywhere.

Unlike the universe, every conversation has a starting point.

Let's Start with a Softball Question

Choose another place and time in history you'd like to live in.

Name every reason why.

In the Struggle Between Happiness and Meaningfulness

Is it better to participate in the grand human social machine *or* seek contentment alone?

Regarding Music Lyrics

Is there anything that hasn't already been said? Any topic at all?

Be Careful Not to Offend Anyone

What would you rather be doing…right now?

Go Back. Way Back

Name a missed opportunity you'd like another shot at.

That Thing Called Love

Purely bio-chemical? A genuine spiritual event? Or a survival mechanism to overcome the perils of being utterly alone?

Play God for 60 Seconds

Suppose you had a red button before you. And suppose pressing this button would utterly, quietly annihilate all the people in the world you consider *evil*.

Would you press it?

Post-Apocalyptic

If society as you know it collapsed tomorrow, how long could you survive?

The Secrets of the Universe

If revealed to you tomorrow, and if they challenged everything you *thought* you knew, could you discard all of your previous beliefs?

Choose your Ending

Set aside your existing belief system. Describe the afterlife as the way you *want* it to be.

Immortality

If and when scientists perfect a method to extend life indefinitely, would *you* take the plunge?

Fork in the Road

Is it better to:

A. Doubt everything. Question the world at every turn. Trust in only what your eyes can see.

B. Be contented by apparent truths. Accept that happiness sometimes comes from *not* knowing.

?

In the Realm of Current Events

Beyond money, why do people choose to be Police Officers? Attorneys? Politicians?

The Straw & the Camel's Back

Describe an event that would drive you to desire vengeance.

Where We're Going, We Don't Need Roads

If, long from now, the world is completely mechanized, thus eliminating the need for most people to work, what will we do with our lives?

In or Out

Which is more mysterious to you:

The ocean deeps?

Or outer space?

Why?

Internet Memes

Cute diversion from the mundane goings on of daily life?

or

Shallow, unfunny result of human boredom?

Autobiography

You've written a book chronicling your life story.

What's the climax?

No Matter how Small

On average, how many lies per month do you tell?

Justify your number.

Completely Unfair

Two fires are raging. You can rush into one house and save your child. Or you can rush into the other and save 100 people. Which house?

Frozen in Time

Think back to the most recent non-selfie photo taken of you.

Caption it.

This One's Rhetorical

Why do so many people get so angry about politics?

Let's Get Physical

Assuming one-on-one combat, what percentage of the world's population could you handle in a fight?

Your Crystal Ball

Consider your life exactly 10 years from today.

Where will you be?

What will you be doing?

Let's Play Dungeons & Dragons

Suppose that when you're born, you have 100 points to spread across three attributes: Intellect, Strength, and Attractiveness

Assign your points.

Explain your choices.

A Moment of Omniscience

If you could ask ONE question of the universe and have it answered utterly and completely, what would it be?

A New Sheriff's in Town

You've just been elected President of a stable, fledgling nation.

You're only allowed to make 3 things illegal.

Name your choices.

Justify them.

All Judgments are Impaired

From the following, choose the worst thing a person could possibly be addicted to: Alcohol, Drugs, Sex, Gambling…or TV…

1 is the Loneliest Number

The world will end tomorrow. Every single human will vanish. You can either save just yourself and carry on alone. Or you can die with everyone else.

Which do you choose?

UFC 666: Jesus versus Superman

If you could lock any two historical figures (dead or alive) in a cage for a fight to the death, which two would you pick?

You: The Director's Cut

If you could choose one song, *just one*, to serve as the soundtrack of your life, which song would it be?

Stepford Wives (And Husbands)

Let's say science perfects an *absolutely* lifelike robot for use as a spouse. And let's say this beautiful, intelligent, *customized-to-you* robot will do anything and everything you ask. Will you buy one?

I’m Just Here so I won’t get Fined

What percentage of Respect is derived from Fear?

That Song by The Clash

A fascinating new planet is discovered far from Earth.
You can journey there safely and live out your life, but it's a one-way ticket for you and whomever you take.
Do you stay or go?

Opinions

A: A sign of human hubris?

B: A natural method of self-expression?

C: An important, inalienable human right?

Back to the Future

You've built a time machine. It only goes one direction in time. Do you want to see how it all *began*? Or how it all will *end*?

To the Victor go the Spoils

On a scale of 1-10, with 10 being absolute agreement and 1 being complete rejection, how would you rate the above statement in terms of whether it's fair or not?

In other words; do the victors deserve the spoils?

Beauty

Truly in the eye of the beholder?

Or not so much?

If a Tree falls and no one Hears

If humanity survives the eons *but* ends at the exact same time as Earth without ever spreading to other planets, define the value of that experience.

Better Lucky than Good?

What percentage of success is due to hard work?

What percentage is due to good fortune?

Switching Sides

It's sometimes said that 1% of the world's people control 99% of the world's wealth.

If you happen to be in the 99%, would you prefer to be with the 1%?

Why?

7 Days

Suppose you are imbued with godlike powers.

And suppose you are given a world to create.

What does this world look like?

Who lives there?

After it's finished, what level of involvement will you have?

Painting with Dreams

Picture yourself in a state of complete and utter contentment.

Where are you?

What are you doing?

Satisfaction

Aside from food, water, and your home, could you live happily from now until the end without buying a single thing more?

Build-a-Mate

Imagine your ideal man or woman sitting across from you. Does he or she have:

A beautiful mind?

A beautiful face?

A beautiful body?

Choose only one.

In the Battle Between

Is there any such thing as absolute good or evil?
Explain your answer.

Line in the Sand

Define the point at which TMI (Too Much Information) is reached.

A word used too often, or not often enough?

Do heroes exist?

If so, define what it takes to be one.

Possible or not?

Can one man's terrorist be another man's freedom fighter?

Or is an enemy just an enemy?

Penny for your Thoughts

If you were hopelessly in love with someone who is taken, would you:

A. Find a subtle way to let them know?
B. Declare yourself and let the cards fall where they may?
C. Forever keep your peace?

Absolute Power…

Assume everyone (or nearly everyone) can be corrupted by one method or another.

What could corrupt *you*?

Skynet Cometh

Do you believe that at any point in the future, human technological advances will cross the line between what is *useful to mankind*, and what is *heretical*?

If so, define that line.

Brimstone or Barbed Wire

Assume there is a Hell.

What does it look it?

Who goes there?

Unshackle the Chains

Consider the laws in whichever country you call home.

Choose three things you want to no longer be illegal.

Museum of ~~Fine~~ Art

At what point does art become so abstract (*ie; not directly derived from any real-world reference)* that it loses meaning for you?

The Caligula Effect

If everyone in the world had as much food, wealth, love, and sex as they desired, would conflict still exist?
And for what reasons?

The Story of You

Refine your experience of life into five single words.

What are they?

Respect

Owed to a fellow human from the get-go?

Or hard earned?

Click

Imagine you possess a remote control capable of fast-forwarding through any part of your life you choose.

Would you use it?

When?

In the Dead of Night

A stranger knocks on your door at midnight.

It's cold and raining. He's hungry and frostbitten.

You have young children.

Would you invite him into your home?

Necromancy

Suppose you've lost a child or a beloved spouse.

But you have a device capable of resurrecting them.

The only cost: you have to kill someone else firsthand.

Use the device?

Or throw it away?

Big Green Men

Pretend you are the general of Earth's armies.
Alien emissaries arrive. They ask to discuss a permanent peace treaty.
However, both the aliens and Earth possess weaponry capable of destroying the other instantaneously. Whoever strikes first, wins.
Pull the trigger?
Or hope for peace?

Food Chain

On a scale of 0-100%, define the value of an animal as compared to a human. (ie; 100% would mean your neighbor's cat is as valuable as your child.)

Does the value change depending on the animal's species?

There will be a Test

If you had to guess (or even make something up) what would you say is the reason for the universe's existence?

100,000 Shades of Grey

Define your personal moral code.

Name something that would make you change it.

The Matrix

If scientists could permanently attach you to a machine that would provide the illusion of a perfect life, would you plug in? What about for only one year?

Don't ask in front of Grandma

Does a 90 year-old human's life possess the same value as a 2 year-old's?

Crimes Against Ourselves

Considering everything done throughout the course of human history, do we deserve to exist?

Metaphorically Speaking

Would you rather:

Serve in Heaven?

Or Reign in Hell?

Fly on the Wall

You've found a black box containing the memories and complete life experiences of another human being. Using it, you can view every moment of that person's existence from start to finish.

Who are you hoping the box belonged to? (e.g., someone famous, a relative, a celebrity, etc.)

The Mind Shovel

Using an implant grafted into your brain, you've been given the power to read minds at will.

How often would you use it?

On whom?

To find what?

BIG Difference

In terms of measurable modern science, celestial bodies such as stars and planets aren't known to be 'alive.'
Assuming this is true, which is more impressive to you:
A single living organism?
Or a massive red giant star?

Far as the Eye can See

Try to imagine what the world will look like in 2,000 years.

Describe it.

Now imagine the world as you *desire* it to look in 2,000 years.

How different are the two?

Robin Hood

Name three situations in which it's acceptable to *steal.*

The Perfect Crime

If you could do *one thing*, one act no matter how dangerous, illegal, or immoral, and get away with it scot free, no repercussions, what would it be?

Gravity of the Situation

You've been given the power to redefine one law of physics however you see fit (e.g., momentum, gravity, force, etc.)
Which law do you choose?
What changes do you make?

Close your Eyes

Imagine a painting that represents your life and your experience of the universe.

What does your painting look like?

Iffy

If you could save 1,000,000 strangers by dying, would you?

What about 1,000?

100?

1?

Boots

Think of all the characters in all the books, movies, plays, and shows you've experienced during your life.
If given the chance, which one would you choose to be?
Why?

Groundhog Day

Imagine you're going to be trapped in time and made to relive the same day over and over again. Forever.

Which day during your life would you choose?

Good Luck

Choose the name of a new color.

It can't look like any existing color in the known spectrum.

Try to describe it without referring to existing colors.

Throw away the Key

What is the worst crime conceivable?

The 3 Best Virtues a Human can Possess are:

____

____

____

Do you possess any of these?

The 3 Worst Flaws a Human can Possess are:

____

____

____

Do you possess any of these?

We All Know One

Is it arrogance if it's true?

Iceberg!

You're on a raft in the middle of the ocean with ten other people.

The water is bone-chillingly cold.

A rescue helicopter will arrive in three hours.

An eleventh person swims up.

If you allow them to climb aboard, there's a 50% chance the raft will capsize and everyone will drown.

Do you allow the eleventh person aboard?

The Hermit

A man lives deep in the mountains. He survives for ninety years, alone and content, but he never travels and never encounters another human being.

Is his life less meaningful than yours?

20/20

Consider all the times in your life you've ever been truly, inconsolably angry.

What percentage of those times did being angry result in a positive solution?

The Love of your Life

Would you rather die after them?

Or before?

Is it Realllly?

The old saying goes: ‘The Pen is Mightier than the Sword.’

True or false?

The Final Frontier

In the modern era, the United States government has allocated as much as 4.41% and as little as 0.49% of its yearly budget to pay for deep space exploration and related sciences.

Given the choice, what percentage would you spend?

Possession

Pretend that *all* objects in the universe are alive. Rocks, water, wind, stars, comets, intergalactic dust, all of it.

And pretend you could inhabit any one of these you choose. You'd live as long as the object did and experience whatever it experienced.

Name your choice.

Camels. Eyes. Needles.

Is it possible for an extremely wealthy person to also be highly virtuous?

Ideas

Can they be killed?

Is it better to…

A. Be skeptical, but immune to disappointment?

B. Be optimistic, and enjoy *possibility*, but suffer devastation when failure occurs?

C. Be stoic, and therefore unaffected whether an outcome is good or bad?

It’s a Texture Thing

Pancakes?

Or waffles?

Not Quite a Cat, but Close

Suppose reincarnation is real, and that each soul completes four terms, each in a different body (animals *or* plants.)
You're currently living your first life-span.
In what form do you hope to live your next three lives?

99 Problems

Which would you rather be:

A slave treated exceedingly well by his masters?

Or a free man struggling to barely survive?

Why?

Your Theory of Everything

Open your imagination to its widest point.
How does everything in the observable universe know what to do?
I.e.; how does an iron atom know it's an iron atom? How does water know to be water?
And so on and so forth.

Think About This One

Does every *single* human life…have value?

And now, the Final Exam

What is *your* Question for Humanity?

Thank you for reading.

It's my hope these 101 questions have entertained, provoked, and challenged you.

The idea came to me while sitting on a couch at a party. In a room full of young, energetic, good-looking people, no one was putting much effort into talking. Everyone was staring at their cell phones.

And so I asked a question.

Then another.

And here we are…

About the author

J Edward Neill became obsessed with writing in early 2001. On one bitterly cold morning in the lowest corridor of his candlelit man-cave, he fingers to keyboard and began hammering away on what would soon become a lifelong obsession. Since that day, he has spent nearly all his free time lost in his daydreams, conjuring ways to write the kind of stories he loved as a child.

When he's not glooming in front of his laptop or iPad, J Edward haunts the internet via his websites: *www.TesseraGuild.com* and *www.DowntheDarkPath.com*. He currently lives in the North Georgia ‘burbs, where he moonlights as a foodie, a sipper of too much pinot noir, and the hugest-armed quarterback never to sniff the NFL.

101 Questions for Humanity is his first non-fiction book.

Also available by J Edward Neill

Novels

Down the Dark Path – Book I in the Tyrants of the Dead trilogy

Dark Moon Daughter – Book II in the Tyrants of the Dead trilogy

Nether Kingdom – Book III in the Tyrants of the Dead trilogy

Hollow Empire – Night of Knives (a serial novel co-authored with John McGuire)

Short Stories

Old Man of Tessera

The Sleepers

Let the Bodies

Non-Fiction

101 Questions for Men

101 Questions for Women

101 Questions for Midnight

101 Sex Questions

444 Questions for the Universe

And coming soon…

Darkness Between the Stars – Prequel to the Tyrants of the Dead trilogy

A Door Never Dreamed Of – Sci-fi novella

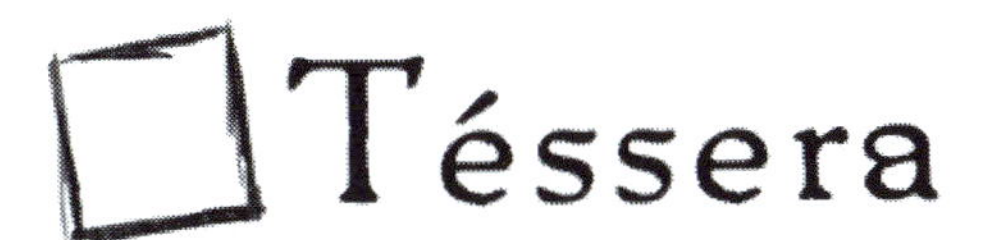

Made in the USA
San Bernardino, CA
24 June 2017